cooking the KOREAN way

Korean dumplings are fun to make and can be eaten alone or with tangy vinegar-soy sauce. (Recipes on pages 18 and 30.)

cooking the KOREAN way

OKWHA CHUNG & JUDY MONROE

PHOTOGRAPHS BY ROBERT L. & DIANE WOLFE

easy menu *ethnic* cookbooks

Lerner Publications Company ▪ Minneapolis

Editor: Vicki Revsbech
Map by J. Michael Roy
Drawings by Jeanette Swofford
Diagram on page 31 by Laura Westlund

Photograph on page 10 courtesy of the Korea
National Tourism Corporation

The publisher wishes to thank Dr. John S. Knapp and Mr. James
E. Laib for their assistance in the preparation of this book.

The page border for this book is based on the crane,
an ancient symbol of longevity in Korea.

With love to my family – O.C.

To Bob, with all my love – J.M.

Library of Congress Cataloging-in-Publication Data

Chung, Okwha.
  Cooking the Korean way.

  (Easy menu ethnic cookbooks)
  Includes index.
  Summary: Introduces the cooking and food habits of Korea,
including such recipes as bean sprout salad and Korean dumplings,
and provides brief information on the geography and history of
the country.
  1. Cookery, Korean—Juvenile literature. 2. Korea—Social life
and customs—Juvenile literature. |1. Cookery, Korean. 2. Korea—
Social life and customs| I. Monroe, Judy. II. Wolfe, Robert L., ill.
III. Wolfe, Diane, ill. IV. Title. V. Series.
TX724.5.K65C59 1988   641.59519   87-4014
ISBN 0-8225-0921-0 (lib. bdg.)

Manufactured in the United States of America

  3 4 5 6 7 8 9 10 97 96 95 94 93 92 91

Tubu tak kogi jjim is as healthy as it is delicious.
(Recipe on page 40.)

CONTENTS

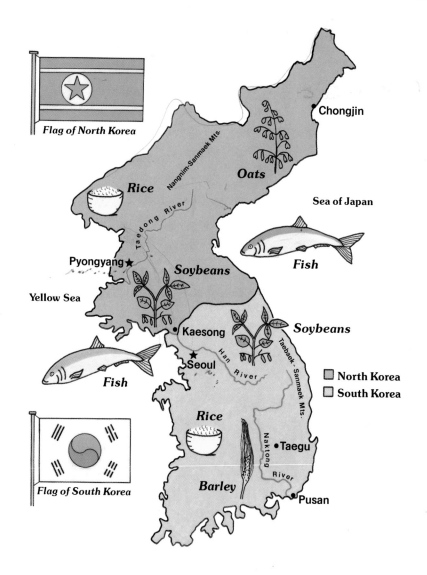

Flag of North Korea

Chongjin

Nangnim-Sanmaek Mts.

Oats

Rice

Taedong River

Sea of Japan

Fish

Pyongyang ★

Soybeans

Yellow Sea

Kaesong

Soybeans

Seoul ★

Han River

Taebaek-Sanmaek Mts.

Fish

North Korea
South Korea

Rice

Naktong

Taegu

Flag of South Korea

Barley

River

Pusan

INTRODUCTION

Korea is a land where the past and the present are often found side by side. Some Koreans live in modern high-rise apartment buildings, while others make their homes in primitive thatched-roof cottages. In the cities, modern skyscrapers shade 500-year-old shrines. Young people honor their elders, and ancient traditions still have an important place in modern Korean society. One of the traditions that has been passed from generation to generation is a varied cuisine that is both healthy and delicious.

THE LAND

The Korean peninsula juts southward from the Asian mainland toward Japan. To the west is the Yellow Sea and to the east is the Sea of Japan. The peninsula shares its northern border with two giants, the Soviet Union and China. Since the 1940s, the Korean peninsula has been divided into two countries, the Democratic People's Republic of Korea, or North Korea, and the Republic of Korea, or South Korea.

Although the entire peninsula is only about the size of the state of Utah, its terrain is varied. Rugged, heavily forested mountains cover most of the inland areas. These regions supply North and South Korea with forest products as well as with minerals. Some of the mighty rivers that flow through the mountains are harnessed to supply electricity.

The mountains give way to gentle, rolling hills and plains on the coasts, except in the southeast, where the Taebaek-Sanmaek Mountains are located. Coastal Korea contains the peninsula's best farmland and is the most heavily populated region. The west coast consists of a network of estuaries and tidal flats, which makes it ideal for growing rice, the most important crop in both North and South Korea. As would be expected of a land with so much coastline, fishing is a thriving business, especially off the eastern coast of North Korea and in the maze of islands and small peninsulas that make up the southern and western coasts of South Korea.

HISTORY

Korea is an ancient land that dates back to about the third century B.C. Although China, Korea's powerful neighbor to the north, has had a great deal of influence on Korean culture, the country has managed to hold on to its independence for most of its 2000-year history.

In the A.D. 600s, a southeastern Korean state called Silla took control of the entire peninsula. The Silla rule lasted for about 200 years, most of them very peaceful and prosperous. By the 900s, however, the government had become very weak and several groups fought for control of the country.

After years of confusion, a general named Wang Kon took over the government of the country and the peninsula was peaceful once again. Wang Kon is probably best remembered for renaming the country Koryo, from which we have derived the word *Korea*. Education and the arts were important to Wang Kon and the Koryo kings that followed him. But this peaceful period was not to last. In the 1200s, Mongol warriors from the north took over the country and controlled it for about 100 years.

After the Mongols were defeated, another general, Yi Songgye, became Koryo's new ruler.

Yi and his descendants ruled the country, which Yi called Choson, from 1392 until 1910. During the Yi dynasty, the peninsula was plagued with constant invasions by the Chinese and Japanese. By the 1600s, the people of Choson were so tired of fighting off their neighbors that they closed the country to foreigners. For 200 years, Koreans lived in isolation from the rest of the world, and their country was known as the Hermit Kingdom.

The 1900s have been a troubled century for Korea. After forcing the Hermit Kingdom to open its ports to other countries in 1876, Japan completely took over the country in 1910. The harsh rule of the Japanese lasted until 1945 when Japan was defeated in World War II. Rather than regaining its freedom after the war, however, the peninsula was occupied by the Soviet Union in the north and by the United States in the south. Because no one was able to agree on who should rule the country, it was split into two separate countries. North Korea was controlled by Communists and South Korea was strongly anti-Communist.

Both North and South Korea wanted to rule the entire peninsula, not just one small part. In 1950, North Korea invaded South Korea. The war that followed lasted three years, but resolved very little. Today, the Korean peninsula is still two separate countries with two very different forms of government.

THE FOOD

Political differences have not prevented the people of North and South Korea from continuing to share a cuisine. Just as Koreans on both sides of the border have a common history, you will find the same kinds of foods and cooking methods in Pyongyang in the north as you will in the southern city of Seoul.

When you sit down to your first Korean meal, you will probably immediately notice the similarities to other Oriental cuisines. Like the Chinese and the Japanese, the Koreans eat with chopsticks, which means that the food is usually cut into bite-sized pieces that are easy to pick up. Many of the ingredients—such as tofu, soy sauce, and a variety of fresh vegetables—as well as some of the cooking methods—including stir-frying, steaming, and braising—are used in other countries in the Far East. But there are also elements of Korean cuisine that make it deliciously different.

Korean food is often highly seasoned, usually with a combination of garlic, ginger, red or black pepper, scallions, soy sauce, sesame seeds, and sesame oil. These dishes are served with a bland grain to cool the heat of the spices. Rice is present at every meal, but you may also find barley, buckwheat, millet, or wheat.

As is true of the rest of the Orient, Koreans eat far less meat than people in other parts of the world. Red meat is scarce in both North and South Korea and is very expensive, so it is usually only served on special occasions. Chicken and fish are more plentiful.

Korean cuisine also offers a vast assortment of vegetarian dishes. Protein-rich soybean products are often eaten instead of meat. The soybean is the main ingredient in tofu, a common meat substitute. This versatile plant is also used to make soybean pastes and sauces, including the slightly sweet Korean soy sauce, which are included in soups and other dishes.

Diners enjoy a meal made up of a wide variety of Korean favorites.

Unlike other Asian cuisines, Korean cuisine includes many uncooked vegetables, frequently served in the form of delicious salads and pickles. The most famous pickle is a spicy Korean staple called kimchi. Like rice, kimchi can be found at every meal.

The cuisine of Korea does not vary widely from region to region. Koreans do try, however, to use the fruits and vegetables that are in season, and they serve heartier fare in the colder months. During the winter, for example, many dishes feature such root vegetables as potatoes and carrots, braised or simmered along with beef or chicken and favorite Korean flavorings.

HOLIDAY FEASTS IN KOREA

Good food is always an important part of any holiday in South Korea, where I was born. Koreans begin the year with a three-day celebration called Sol. Sol is a time to greet the new year and to show respect for elders. My mother would serve many kinds of sweet and savory cakes, rice soup, egg rolls, meat dumplings, fried fish, broiled beef, kimchi, sweetened rice, candied lotus root and ginger, date balls, chestnut balls, and fresh fruit.

The first full moon of the year is an ancient day of worship. We kept torches burning all night long. Some people set off firecrackers and cracked nuts to scare off evil spirits. Every year, we would eat a special dish of rice, millet, corn, and red beans. We also ate vegetables and various nuts, especially chestnuts, pinenuts, and walnuts.

I always looked forward to Shampoo Day, or Yadu Nal, on June 15th. My family would visit with friends next to a stream or a waterfall, and later we would bathe in the clear water to ward off fevers for the rest of the year. Our delicious picnic meal included dumplings, sweet cakes, grilled fish, and watermelon.

In autumn, we celebrated the harvest season with a day of thanksgiving called Chusok. We would eat a wonderful meal that included fruits and vegetables of the season, rice cakes, and taro soup. Autumn was also the time to prepare our kimchi for the winter.

Kimchi is a pickle made of cabbage and a variety of other vegetables. Our kimchi consisted of cabbage, turnips, radishes, and cucumbers and was seasoned with scallions, garlic, red pepper, and ginger root. For a special touch, my mother would sometimes chop in bits of salty fish or shrimp. Each year after the kimchi was assembled, we would place it in large jars and leave it to ferment for weeks. Some of our kimchi was very spicy, while other jars held milder versions. It is traditional to bury jars full of kimchi in the ground to maintain the correct temperature until the pickle is ready to eat.

When you try the recipes in this book, keep in mind that appearance is as important as flavor in Korean cooking. A good Korean cook will be very careful to cut food into even pieces and try to include five colors at every meal: red, green, yellow, white, and black. This attention to detail makes every meal a festive occasion.

BEFORE YOU BEGIN

Cooking any dish, plain or fancy, is easier and more fun if you are familiar with its ingredients. Korean cooking makes use of some ingredients that you may not know. You should also be familiar with the special terms that will be used in various recipes in this book. Therefore, *before* you start cooking any of the dishes in this book, study the following "dictionary" of special ingredients and terms very carefully. Then read through each recipe you want to try from beginning to end.

Now you are ready to shop for ingredients and to organize the cookware you will need. Once you have assembled everything, you can begin to cook. It is also very important to read *The Careful Cook* on page 44 before you start. Following these rules will make your cooking experience safe, fun, and easy.

COOKING UTENSILS

charcoal grill – A cooker in which charcoal provides the heat and food is placed on a metal grate above the coals

colander – A bowl-shaped dish with holes in it that is used for washing or draining food

pastry brush – A small brush with nylon bristles used for coating food with melted butter or other liquids

skewer – A thin wooden or metal stick used to hold small pieces of meat or vegetables for broiling or grilling

steamer — A utensil designed for cooking food with steam. Oriental steamers have tight-fitting lids and grates or racks for holding the food.

tongs — A scissor-shaped utensil used to grasp food

wok — A pot with a rounded bottom and sloping sides, ideally suited for stir-fried dishes. A large frying pan will work as a substitute.

COOKING TERMS

beat — To stir rapidly in a circular motion

boil — To heat a liquid over high heat until bubbles form and rise rapidly to the surface

broil — To cook directly under a heat source so that the side of the food facing the heat cooks rapidly

chill — To refrigerate a food until it is cold

fillet — A boneless piece of fish or meat

fluff — To gently separate small pieces of food, such as rice, that have packed down

garnish — To decorate with a small piece of food

grill — To cook over hot charcoal

marinate — To soak food in a liquid in order to add flavor and to tenderize it

preheat — To allow an oven to warm up to a certain temperature before putting food in it

sauté — To fry quickly over high heat in oil or fat, stirring or turning the food to prevent burning

seed — To remove seeds from a food

shred — To tear or cut into small pieces, either by hand or with a grater

simmer — To cook over low heat in liquid kept just below its boiling point

steam — To cook food with the steam from boiling water

stir-fry — To quickly cook bite-sized pieces of food in a small amount of oil over high heat

toss — To lightly mix pieces of food together

SPECIAL INGREDIENTS

bean sprouts – Sprouts from the mung bean. They can be bought either canned or fresh.

black mushrooms – Dried, fragrant mushrooms available at Oriental groceries

cayenne pepper – Ground hot red pepper

cellophane noodles – Thin noodles made from mung beans

Chinese cabbage – A pale green vegetable with broad, tightly packed leaves. Also called celery cabbage or napa cabbage.

crushed red pepper flakes – Dried pieces of hot red peppers used to give a spicy flavor to food

ginger root – A knobby, light brown root used to flavor foods

oyster sauce – A sauce made from oysters, sugar, and soy sauce. It is sometimes used in place of soy sauce in Oriental cooking.

romaine lettuce – A lettuce with long, crisp upright leaves

sesame oil – The oil pressed from sesame seeds

sesame seeds – Seeds from an herb grown in tropical countries. They are often toasted before they are eaten.

soy sauce – A dark brown sauce made from soybeans and other ingredients that is used to flavor Oriental foods

tofu – A processed curd made from soybeans

wonton skins – Small, thin squares of soft dough made from flour, water, and eggs. They can be bought frozen or refrigerated.

EATING WITH CHOPSTICKS

Chopsticks are not difficult to manage once you have learned the basic technique. The key to using them is to hold the inside stick still while moving the outside stick back and forth. The pair then acts as pincers to pick up pieces of food.

Hold the thicker end of the first chopstick in the crook of your thumb, resting the lower part lightly against the inside of your ring finger.

Then put the second chopstick between the tips of your index and middle fingers and hold it with your thumb, much as you would hold a pencil.

Now you can make the outer chopstick move by bending your index and middle fingers toward the inside chopstick. The tips of the two sticks should come together like pincers when you bend your fingers. Once you get a feel for the technique, just keep practicing. Soon you'll be an expert!

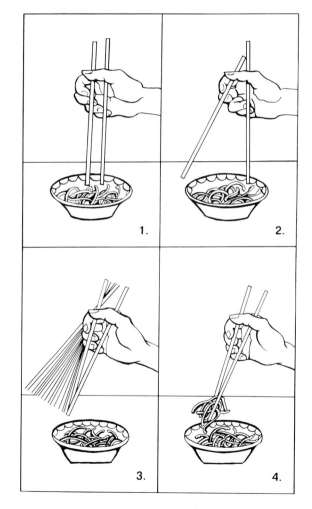

A KOREAN MENU

There are very few, if any, differences between breakfast, lunch, and dinner in Korea. A typical meal consists of rice, soup, kimchi, vegetables, and broiled or grilled meat or fish. Koreans seldom serve dessert, but often eat fresh fruit.

Plan your Korean menu by choosing dishes from the groups below. For breakfast, which is often the biggest meal of the day, you might try cold cucumber soup, steamed stuffed peppers, and fish patties. Lunch could consist of potato soup and mixed vegetables with cellophane noodles. For a hearty dinner, serve beef short rib soup, mixed vegetable salad, and steamed chicken. Of course, rice and kimchi can be eaten at any meal, any time of the day. You can also make up your own combinations. For an authentic Korean meal, try to include the colors red, green, yellow, white, and black. Contrasts are important, so serve bland rice with a spicy dish, or a cold salad with a hot soup. Use your imagination and these Korean dishes will become favorites you will serve again and again.

ENGLISH	*KOREAN*	*PRONUNCIATION GUIDE*
Staples	**Ju shik**	joo shik
Toasted Sesame Seeds	Kkae sogūm	gay so-gum
Vinegar-soy Sauce	Ch'o kanjang	cho kahn-jahng
White Rice	Hin pap	heen pop
Noodles	Kuk su	kook soo
Kimchi and Salads	**Kimch'i, Namul**	kim-chee, nah-mool
Kimchi	Kimch'i	kim-chee
Bean Sprout Salad	Sukju namul	sook-joo nah-mool
Mixed Vegetable Salad	Sukju oi namul	sook-joo oh-ee nah-mool
Spinach Salad	Shigūmch'i namul	shee-guhm-chee nah-mool

ENGLISH	KOREAN	PRONUNCIATION GUIDE
Soups	**Guk**	gook
Cold Cucumber Soup	Oi naeng guk	oh-ee nayng gook
Potato Soup	Kamja guk	kahm-jah gook
Beef Short Rib Soup	Kalbi guk	kahl-bee gook
Fried, Stir-fried, and Grilled Dishes	**T'wigim, Pokkŭm, Kui**	twee-gim, poh-guhm, goo-ee
Fish Patties	Saeng sŏn jŏn	sayng sawn jawn
Deep-fried Chicken Wings	Tak nalgae t'wigim	tahk nahl-gay twee-gim
Korean Dumplings	Mandu	mahn-doo
Mixed Vegetables with Cellophane Noodles	Chap ch'ae	chop chay
Grilled Beef with Vegetables	San jŏk	sahn jawk
Barbecued Beef	Pulgogi	pool-go-gee
Simmered and Steamed Dishes	**Jjim**	jim
Simmered Beef Short Ribs	Kalbi jjim	kahl-bee jim
Simmered Pork	Che yuk	chay yook
Simmered Chicken	Tak jjim	tahk jim
Steamed Chicken with Tofu	Tubu tak kogi jjim	too-boo tahk ko-gee jim
Steamed Stuffed Peppers	Ko ch'u jjim	ko choo jim
Egg Custard with Meatballs	Al jjim	ahl jim

STAPLES

Toasted Sesame Seeds/ Kkae sogŭm

The delicious, nutty flavor of sesame seeds is heightened when the seeds are lightly toasted and crushed. Toasted sesame seeds are usually made in large quantities because they are found in so many Korean recipes. If you like, you can add a pinch of salt to the sesame seeds as you crush them.

2 tablespoons sesame seeds

1. Place sesame seeds in a small frying pan. (Do not add oil.) Cook, stirring constantly, over medium heat 2 to 4 minutes or until golden brown. (Be careful not to burn.) Remove from heat and set aside to cool.
2. Pour toasted seeds into a large bowl and crush with the back of a wooden spoon.

Makes 2 tablespoons

Vinegar-soy Sauce/ Ch'o kanjang

This light dipping sauce has a sour and salty flavor that goes well with meat, vegetables, and fried food.

4 tablespoons soy sauce
3 tablespoons vinegar
1 teaspoon sugar
**1 teaspoon finely chopped
    green onions**
1 teaspoon toasted sesame seeds

1. Combine all ingredients in a small bowl. Stir to dissolve sugar.
2. Vinegar-soy sauce will keep for up to a week refrigerated in a tightly covered glass container.

Makes ½ cup

White Rice/
Hin pap

For centuries, Koreans have served white rice at every meal, either alone or combined with such foods as barley, millet, corn, beans, or wheat. This recipe is made with the short-grain rice that Koreans prefer, which is tender and a little sticky.

2 cups short-grain white rice
2⅔ cups water

1. In a deep saucepan, bring rice and water to a boil over high heat. Boil, uncovered, for 2 to 3 minutes.
2. Cover pan, reduce heat to low, and simmer rice 20 to 25 minutes or until all water is absorbed.
3. Remove pan from heat. Keep covered and let rice steam 10 minutes.
4. Fluff with a fork and serve hot.

Serves 4

Noodles/
Kuk su

Noodles are a versatile staple food that can be added to soups or to stir-fried, steamed, or simmered dishes. A wide variety of noodles, both thick and thin, are used in Korean cooking. This recipe can be made with wheat, buckwheat, or cellophane noodles.

3 cups water
½ pound noodles

1. In a large saucepan, bring water to a boil over high heat. Add noodles and return to a boil.
2. Reduce heat to medium-high and cook noodles, uncovered, for 5 to 7 minutes or until soft.
3. Drain noodles in a colander and rinse briefly in cold water. Serve immediately.

Serves 4

KIMCHI AND SALADS

Korean salads, or *namul,* are probably very different from the salads you are used to. *Namul* usually feature fresh or lightly cooked vegetables such as bean sprouts, carrots, cabbage, and cucumbers. But unlike most salads, *namul* can be very spicy and are eaten in very small portions with rice. Cabbage is also the main ingredient in the spicy Korean pickle called kimchi.

Kimchi/Kimch'i

Kimchi is the Korean national dish that is found at every meal. There are dozens of variations of this famous pickle, which range from mild to very spicy. You can make a simple kimchi from cabbage alone, or you can substitute any combination of turnips, radishes, and cucumber for all or part of the cabbage. Salted fish or shrimp can also be added. Remember, the longer kimchi sits, the spicier it will be.

5 cups cabbage, cut into bite-sized pieces
6 tablespoons salt
2 tablespoons sugar
1 teaspoon to 2 tablespoons crushed red pepper flakes
¼ teaspoon finely chopped ginger root
1 clove garlic, peeled and finely chopped
2 green onions, finely chopped

1. In a large colander, mix cabbage with 5 tablespoons salt. Let sit for 3 hours.
2. Rinse cabbage thoroughly 2 or 3 times. Gently squeeze out excess liquid with your hands.
3. Place the drained cabbage in a large glass bowl. Add the remaining ingredients and mix thoroughly.
4. Cover cabbage mixture tightly with plastic wrap and let sit at room temperature for 1 or 2 days.
5. Chill kimchi before serving.

Makes 5 cups

Spinach salad *(front right)*, **mixed vegetable salad** *(back left)*, **and bean sprout salad** *(back right)*, **are tasty additions to a Korean meal, which wouldn't be complete without the spicy pickle called kimchi** *(front left)*.

Bean Sprout Salad/
Sukju namul

Bean sprouts are the white, crunchy shoots of the mung bean that are often used in Korean soups and stir-fries. Soybean sprouts, which have a stronger taste and smell than the sprouts from the mung bean, can be used in this recipe if they are cooked a minute or two longer.

3 cups water
3 cups bean sprouts
½ teaspoon soy sauce
2 teaspoons vinegar
1 teaspoon sesame oil
1 teaspoon sugar
¼ teaspoon salt
⅛ teaspoon black pepper
⅛ teaspoon cayenne pepper
2 green onions, finely chopped
1 teaspoon toasted sesame seeds
     (recipe on page 18)

1. In a large saucepan, bring water to a boil over high heat. Add bean sprouts, reduce heat to medium, and cook for 2 to 3 minutes or until crisp-tender.
2. Pour bean sprouts into a colander and rinse with cold water. Drain well and place in a large bowl.
3. In a small bowl, combine remaining ingredients and stir to dissolve sugar.
4. Pour dressing over bean sprouts, toss, and serve.

Serves 4

Mixed Vegetable Salad/
Sukju oi namul

To make this salad more colorful, add one medium carrot that has been shredded.

1 medium cucumber, peeled
½ cup vinegar
1 tablespoon plus 1½ teaspoons salt
1½ cups water
1½ cups bean sprouts
1 tablespoon sesame oil
1 green onion, finely chopped
1 tablespoon toasted sesame seeds
     (recipe on page 18)

1. Cut cucumber in half lengthwise and scoop out seeds with a spoon. Slice into thin half rounds.
2. In a medium bowl, combine vinegar and 1 tablespoon salt. Add cucumber, mix well, and set aside for 15 minutes.
3. In a large saucepan, bring water to a boil over high heat. Add bean sprouts, reduce heat to medium, and cook 2 to 3 minutes or until crisp-tender.
4. Pour bean sprouts into a colander and rinse with cold water. Drain well and place in a large bowl.
5. Pour cucumber mixture into colander and gently squeeze out excess liquid with hands.
6. Add cucumber mixture to bean sprouts and toss. Add sesame oil, green onions, sesame seeds, and 1½ teaspoons salt and toss again.
7. Refrigerate 1 to 2 hours before serving.

Serves 4

Spinach Salad/
Shigŭmch'i namul

This delicious salad features three of the most popular ingredients in Korean cooking: soy sauce, sesame seeds, and garlic.

½ **cup water**
1 **pound fresh spinach, cleaned**
2 **teaspoons soy sauce**
1 **tablespoon sesame oil**
½ **teaspoon finely chopped garlic**
1 **tablespoon toasted sesame seeds (recipe on page 18)**

1. In a large saucepan, bring water to a boil over high heat. Add spinach, cover, and reduce heat to medium-high. Cook for 2 to 3 minutes or until bright green. Drain in a colander.
2. When cool, gently squeeze out excess water with your hands. Cut spinach into 2-inch lengths and place in a large bowl.
3. Add remaining ingredients and mix well. Serve at room temperature.

Serves 4

Korean soups can be light and delicately flavored like cold cucumber soup *(left)* **and potato soup** *(right)* **or hearty and filling like beef short rib soup** *(center).*

SOUPS

Soup can be served as a main dish at any Korean meal, including breakfast. Most soup stock is made from beef, but fish or chicken is also occasionally used. There are two categories of soup: light, clear soups seasoned with soy sauce or salt, and hearty soups that are often made with soybean paste. Traditionally, clear soups are served in the morning, and the heartier soups are for lunch or dinner.

Cold Cucumber Soup/ Oi naeng guk

Although you can find the cucumber all over the world, it originated in southern Asia. This soup is often served in the summer because the cucumber's crisp, refreshing taste stimulates faded hot-weather appetites. Koreans sometimes add toasted seaweed.

2 medium cucumbers, peeled
1 tablespoon soy sauce
2 tablespoons vinegar

4 teaspoons salt
1 green onion, finely chopped
1 tablespoon toasted sesame seeds (recipe on page 18)
4 cups cold water
dash cayenne pepper (optional)
3 or 4 ice cubes (optional)

1. Cut cucumbers in half lengthwise and scoop out seeds with a spoon. Slice into thin half rounds.
2. In a large bowl, combine cucumbers, soy sauce, vinegar, salt, green onions, and sesame seeds. Set aside to marinate for 30 minutes.
3. Add water and stir well. Refrigerate 1 to 2 hours.
4. Before serving, sprinkle with cayenne pepper and add 3 or 4 ice cubes to keep soup cold.

Serves 4

Potato Soup/
Kamja guk

Try eating potato soup the way the Koreans do—for breakfast. You can also add bite-sized pieces of onion and chunks of tofu.

2 10¾ ounce cans (about 3 cups) beef
    or chicken broth
2 large potatoes, peeled and cut
    into bite-sized pieces
2 medium carrots, peeled and cut
    into bite-sized pieces
½ cup quartered mushrooms
1 green onion, chopped
⅛ teaspoon black pepper

1. In a large saucepan, combine broth, potatoes, and carrots. Bring to a boil over high heat, cover, and reduce heat to low. Cook for 10 minutes or until vegetables are tender.
2. Add mushrooms, green onions, and black pepper. Stir well and cook 2 minutes more.
3. Serve hot.

Serves 4

Beef Short Rib Soup/
Kalbi guk

This hearty family favorite is only served for dinner. For variety, cellophane noodles may also be added.

1½ pounds beef short ribs
4 cups water
1 teaspoon salt
1 tablespoon soy sauce
1 teaspoon sesame oil
1 clove garlic, peeled and crushed
1 green onion, finely chopped
1 teaspoon toasted sesame seeds
    (recipe on page 18)

1. Place meat, water, and salt in a large saucepan. Bring to a boil over high heat, cover, and reduce heat to low. Cook about 2 hours or until meat is tender.
2. Just before serving, add soy sauce, sesame oil, garlic, green onions, and sesame seeds. Mix well and cook 2 minutes more.
3. Serve hot.

Serves 4

FRIED, STIR-FRIED, AND GRILLED DISHES

Koreans prefer to use very little oil in their cooking, even when frying or stir-frying. Stir-frying is a favorite way to cook vegetables because they remain crisp and colorful. Because it is such a quick cooking method, be sure to have all your ingredients chopped and ready before you start to stir-fry.

Some of the most popular Korean dishes are charcoal grilled, a delicious way to cook meat. Although the flavor will be a little different, you can also broil these dishes.

Fish Patties/
Saeng sŏn jŏn

With water on three sides, it is not surprising that fish is an important part of Korean cuisine. For this recipe, you can use sole, cod, haddock, or any other whitefish. If you use frozen fish, be sure it is completely thawed before mixing it with the other ingredients.

2 eggs, beaten
½ teaspoon salt
⅛ teaspoon black pepper
⅛ teaspoon finely chopped garlic
2 tablespoons finely chopped green onions, green part only
1 cup chopped fish fillets
1 tablespoon vegetable oil

1. Combine eggs, salt, black pepper, garlic, green onions, and fish in a large bowl and mix well.
2. In a wok or large frying pan, heat oil over high heat for 1 minute. Drop tablespoons of the fish mixture into oil to make 2-inch patties and fry 2 minutes per side or until set and starting to turn brown.
3. Serve hot with vinegar-soy sauce (recipe on page 18) and rice.

Serves 4

Deep-fried Chicken Wings/
Tak nalgae t'wigim

This is just one of the many ways to prepare chicken Korean-style. The chicken wings can also be baked in a 350° oven for 30 minutes. For a slightly different flavor, substitute honey for the sugar and add a sprinkling of toasted sesame seeds.

10 chicken wings
½ cup flour
½ cup vegetable oil
⅓ cup soy sauce
1 teaspoon lemon juice
2 teaspoons oyster sauce
2 tablespoons sugar
**1 clove garlic, peeled and
     finely chopped**
⅛ teaspoon finely chopped ginger root

1. Cut off and discard the tips of the wings and separate each wing into 3 pieces.
2. Pour flour into a large plastic bag. Add chicken pieces, twist bag closed, and shake until chicken is completely coated with flour.
3. In a wok or large frying pan, heat oil over medium heat for 1 minute. Carefully place 4 or 5 pieces of chicken into oil with tongs and fry about 4 to 5 minutes or until all sides are golden brown. Keep warm in a 200° oven while you fry the remaining chicken.
4. Combine remaining ingredients in a large saucepan and bring to a boil over high heat. Remove from heat, add chicken wings, and stir to coat wings with sauce.
5. Serve hot with rice.

Serves 4

Both deep-fried chicken wings *(back)* and fish patties *(front)* are cooked quickly so they absorb very little oil and keep their fresh flavor.

Korean Dumplings/ Mandu

These wonderful deep-fried dumplings are usually served at winter celebrations. In Korea, the wrappers are made by hand, a task that takes skill and patience.

¼ **pound ground beef**
1 **cup plus 1 tablespoon vegetable oil**
½ **small onion, peeled and finely chopped**
¾ **cup cabbage, shredded**
½ **cup bean sprouts, chopped**
1 **green onion, finely chopped**
1½ **teaspoons salt**
   dash black pepper
25 **wonton skins**
1 **egg**

1. In a large frying pan or wok, cook meat until brown, mashing with a fork to break into small pieces. Drain off fat and set meat aside.
2. Wash pan and dry thoroughly.
3. Heat 1 tablespoon vegetable oil over high heat for 1 minute. Add onions and sauté 2 to 3 minutes or until crisp-tender.
4. Add cabbage and continue to cook, stirring frequently, for another 2 to 3 minutes or until cabbage is crisp-tender.
5. Add bean sprouts and green onions, mix well, and cook for 1 to 2 minutes more.
6. Remove pan from heat and pour vegetable mixture into a colander to drain off excess liquid.
7. In a large bowl, combine meat, vegetables, salt, and black pepper and mix well.
8. Place 1 wonton skin on a flat surface. Cover remaining skins with a slightly damp kitchen towel (not terry cloth) so they won't dry out. Fold according to directions on page 31.
9. In a large frying pan or wok, heat 1 cup vegetable oil over medium heat for 1 minute. Carefully place 6 dumplings into oil with tongs and fry 3 to 4 minutes or until golden brown. Turn and fry other side 2 to 3 minutes. Keep fried dumplings warm in a 200° oven.

Makes 25 dumplings

HOW TO FOLD DUMPLINGS

1. Have ready 1 beaten egg and a pastry brush. Brush all 4 edges of skin with beaten egg.
2. Place about 1 tablespoon of filling mixture just above center of skin.
3. Fold skin in half over filling to form triangle and press edges together to seal.
4. Repeat with remaining skins.

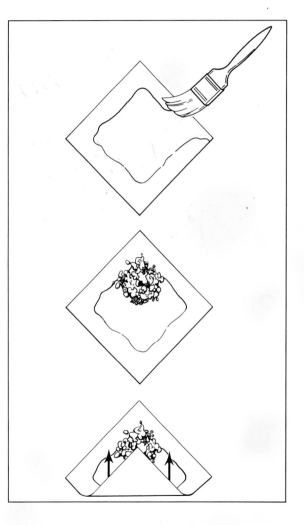

This dish, called *chap ch'ae* in Korean, features cellophane noodles, an oriental staple made from mung beans.

Mixed Vegetables with Cellophane Noodles/ Chap ch'ae

Found throughout Korea, this popular dish can also be prepared with thinly sliced beef.

5 dried black mushrooms
1 cup hot water
4 tablespoons soy sauce
2 teaspoons sugar
½ teaspoon finely chopped garlic
4 teaspoons toasted sesame seeds
   (recipe on page 18)
1 chicken breast, skinned, boned and
   cut into bite-sized pieces
2 ounces cellophane noodles
6 tablespoons vegetable oil
1 large onion, peeled and chopped
3 to 4 medium carrots, peeled and cut
   into thin 2-inch strips
1 cup bean sprouts
½ cup fresh spinach, cleaned and
   chopped
5 teaspoons sesame oil

1. In a small bowl, soak mushrooms in hot water for 20 minutes or until soft. Drain well and chop, discarding stems.
2. In a medium bowl, combine 2 tablespoons soy sauce, 1 teaspoon sugar, garlic, 2 teaspoons sesame seeds, and chicken. Set aside.
3. Cook and drain noodles according to recipe on page 19. With a sharp knife or scissors, cut noodles into 3-inch lengths. Place in a large bowl and set aside.
4. In a large frying pan or wok, heat 1 tablespoon vegetable oil over high heat for 1 minute. Add chicken and fry, stirring frequently, for 2 to 3 minutes or until white and tender. Remove pan from heat and add chicken to noodles.
5. Wash the pan and dry thoroughly.
6. Heat 1 tablespoon vegetable oil over high heat for 1 minute. Add mushrooms and cook, stirring frequently, for 1 minute or until soft. Remove from pan and add to noodles. Repeat with remaining vegetables, cooking each one separately. You will not need to wash the pan between vegetables.

7. Add 2 tablespoons soy sauce, 1 teaspoon sugar, 2 teaspoons sesame seeds and 5 teaspoons sesame oil to noodle mixture and mix thoroughly.
8. Serve warm or at room temperature with rice.

Serves 4

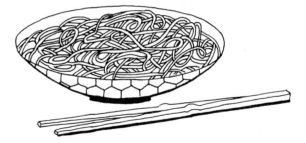

Grilled Beef with Vegetables/
San jŏk

These colorful skewers of meat and vege-
tables are served during festive occasions,
and they are especially loved by Korean
children. Vary the green peppers with green
onions or Chinese peapods. If you prefer,
you can fry the skewers in a little vegetable
oil instead of grilling or broiling them.

½ **cup soy sauce**
2 **tablespoons sugar**
¼ **teaspoon black pepper**
½ **teaspoon finely chopped garlic**
1 **pound sirloin tip, thinly sliced into**
   ½- by 2-inch pieces
3 **or 4 medium carrots, peeled and**
   cut into ¼- by 2-inch pieces
1 **cup mushrooms, cut in half**
1 **large green pepper, seeded and cut**
   into 2- by 2-inch pieces
1 **medium onion, peeled and cut into**
   2- by 2-inch pieces

1. In a medium bowl, combine ¼ cup soy sauce, 1 tablespoon sugar, ⅛ teaspoon black pepper, and ¼ teaspoon garlic. Add meat, mix well, and set aside for 15 minutes.
2. In a shallow bowl, combine the remaining soy sauce, sugar, black pepper, and garlic, and set aside.
3. Preheat oven to broil or have an adult start the charcoal grill.
4. Thread 1 piece of meat onto skewer, then 1 piece of carrot, 1 piece of mushroom, 1 piece of green pepper, and 1 piece of onion. Repeat meat/carrot/mushroom/ green pepper/onion sequence until 4 skewers are filled.
5. Dip the filled skewers into the sauce, turning to coat all sides.
6. Broil or grill the meat and vegetables 4 to 5 minutes or until meat is brown, turning often so that all sides are cooked evenly.
7. Serve hot from skewers.

Serves 4

Pulgogi (left), which is sometimes served wrapped in lettuce leaves, and colorful grilled beef with vegetables *(right)* are two festive ways to serve beef.

Barbecued Beef/ Pulgogi

Next to kimchi, pulgogi *may be Korea's best-known dish. Thin strips of spicy beef are cooked over a* pulgogi, *a dome-shaped charcoal grill. Although it is often eaten during the summer as picnic fare, this dish is good any time. Thinly sliced pork loin can be substituted for the beef.*

4 tablespoons soy sauce
2 tablespoons sesame oil
2 tablespoons sugar
½ teaspoon black pepper
1 clove garlic, peeled and finely chopped
4 tablespoons finely chopped green onions
1 tablespoon toasted sesame seeds (recipe on page 18)
1½ pounds sirloin tip, thinly sliced into ½- by 2-inch pieces
12 romaine lettuce leaves (optional)
1 cup cooked rice (optional)
⅛ teaspoon cayenne pepper (optional)

1. In a large bowl, combine soy sauce, sesame oil, sugar, black pepper, garlic, green onions, and sesame seeds. Add meat and mix well. Cover and refrigerate 1 to 2 hours.
2. Preheat oven to broil or have an adult start the charcoal grill.
3. Broil or grill meat for 2 to 3 minutes per side or until brown.
4. Serve with vegetable side dishes and rice; or place meat on lettuce leaves with 2 teaspoons hot rice and a dash of cayenne pepper per leaf and roll up leaf. (See photo on p. 35.)

Serves 4

SIMMERED AND STEAMED DISHES

In Korea, simmering and steaming are the two most popular ways to cook meats and root vegetables. Simmered dishes are made by adding liquid and seasonings to a pot of meat and cooking the mixture for an hour or two over very low heat. Sometimes vegetables are added during the last half hour of cooking. Steamed dishes are cooked over boiling water, a method that keeps food fresh-tasting and attractive and also helps it to retain most of its nutrients.

Simmered Beef Short Ribs/Kalbi jjim

In Korea, simmered beef short ribs are prepared for festive occasions, particularly birthdays and New Year's celebrations. This colorful winter dish is popular with the cook because it is so easy to make.

½ **cup water**
2½ **pounds lean beef short ribs,**
    separated into pieces
½ **cup soy sauce**
2 **teaspoons sesame oil**
¼ **cup sugar**
½ **teaspoon black pepper**
1 **clove garlic, peeled and chopped**
1 **small onion, peeled and chopped**
2 **large carrots, peeled and chopped**
3½ **teaspoons toasted sesame seeds**
    (recipe on page 18)
3 **green onions, finely chopped**
5 **mushrooms, cut in half**

1. Combine water and meat in a large saucepan and bring to a boil over high heat. Reduce heat to medium, cover, and cook, stirring occasionally, for 1½ hours or until meat is tender.
2. Add soy sauce, sesame oil, sugar, black pepper, garlic, onions, carrots, and 2½ teaspoons sesame seeds and stir well. Cover, reduce heat to low, and cook about 30 minutes or until vegetables are tender.
3. Add green onions and mushrooms and cook 1 to 2 minutes more.
4. Garnish with remaining sesame seeds.

Serves 4

Simmered chicken *(front),* **simmered beef short ribs** *(back left),* **and simmered pork** *(back right)* are cooked very slowly over low heat until the meat is tender and flavorful.

Simmered Pork/
Che yuk

While the meat in this dish slowly simmers, it absorbs the delicate flavor of ginger. A Korean favorite, simmered pork is often served with salty shrimp.

2½ **cups water**
1 **teaspoon salt**
2 **½- by 1-inch pieces ginger root**
1½ **pounds boneless pork loin, excess fat removed**

1. In a large saucepan, combine water, salt, and ginger. Add pork, cover, and bring to a boil over high heat.
2. Reduce heat to low and cook pork, covered, for 1½ hours or until tender.
3. Cool pork to room temperature and cut into thin slices.
4. Serve with vinegar-soy sauce (recipe on page 18) and rice.

Serves 4

Simmered Chicken/
Tak jjim

To vary this tasty and easy dish, add carrots, potatoes, or soaked black mushrooms with the tough stems removed.

2 **tablespoons soy sauce**
1 **tablespoon sesame oil**
1 **tablespoon sugar**
⅛ **teaspoon salt**
⅛ **teaspoon black pepper**
¼ **teaspoon crushed red pepper flakes**
8 **chicken legs or thighs, skinned, boned, and cut into 1½-inch pieces**
1 **clove garlic, peeled and finely chopped**
1 **medium onion, peeled and chopped**
1 **green onion, chopped**

1. Combine all ingredients in a large saucepan and mix thoroughly. Refrigerate for 2 to 3 hours.
2. Cook over low heat, covered, for 1 hour or until chicken is tender.

Serves 4

Steamed Chicken with Tofu/Tubu tak kogi jjim

Although much of Korean cooking is based on tradition, new flavors are also welcomed. This recipe uses ketchup, a fairly recent addition to Korean cuisine.

⅓ cup soy sauce
3 tablespoons ketchup
⅛ teaspoon black pepper
⅛ teaspoon finely chopped ginger
1 clove garlic, peeled and crushed
1 green onion, finely chopped
3 to 4 medium carrots, peeled and
　　cut into bite-sized pieces
½ cup mushrooms, quartered
½ medium green pepper, seeded and
　　cut into bite-sized pieces
6 chicken legs or thighs, skinned and
　　boned, and cut into 1½-inch pieces
½ cup tofu, drained and cut into 1-inch
　　cubes

1. Combine all ingredients in a large heat-resistant bowl and mix well.
2. Pour ½ cup water into a steamer or large kettle and place bowl containing chicken mixture in water.
3. Bring water to a boil over high heat. Reduce heat to medium, cover pan, and steam for 20 to 25 minutes or until chicken is tender.
4. Serve hot with rice.

Serves 4

Steamed Stuffed Peppers/ Ko ch'u jjim

This recipe contains tofu, a high-protein food made from soybeans that is found in many Korean dishes. The versatile soybean, which has been an important crop in the Orient for about 5,000 years, is also used to make flour, oil, and vegetable-based cheese and milk.

¾ cup tofu
½ pound ground beef or ground pork
1 teaspoon salt
⅛ teaspoon black pepper
**1 clove garlic, peeled and finely
    chopped**
1 green onion, finely chopped
**1 teaspoon toasted sesame seeds
    (recipe on page 18)**
**4 small green peppers, cut in half
    lengthwise and seeded**

1. Squeeze out water from tofu with hands. Place in a large bowl and mash with a fork.
2. Add meat, salt, black pepper, garlic, green onions, and sesame seeds and mix well.
3. Fill each green pepper half with meat-tofu mixture.
4. Place stuffed green peppers on a pie plate. Pour ½ cup water into a steamer or large kettle and place pie plate in water.
5. Bring water to a boil over high heat. Reduce heat to medium, cover pan, and steam for 20 to 25 minutes or until meat is brown.
6. Serve hot with vinegar-soy sauce (recipe on page 18) and rice.

Serves 4

Egg Custard
with Meatballs/
Al jjim

Often served for breakfast during the winter, this dish is also found on the dinner table. It can be steamed in four small heat-resistant bowls to make individual servings.

¼ **pound ground beef**
½ **teaspoon soy sauce**
1 **teaspoon sesame oil**
⅛ **teaspoon black pepper**
1 **green onion, finely chopped**
1 **teaspoon finely chopped onion**
1 **tablespoon toasted sesame seeds**
　　(recipe on page 18)
4 **large eggs**
¼ **cup water**
⅛ **teaspoon cayenne pepper**

1. In a large bowl, combine meat, soy sauce, sesame oil, black pepper, green onions, onions, and sesame seeds. Mix thoroughly with hands. Form into 20 1-inch meatballs.

2. In a large heat-resistant bowl, beat together eggs, water, and cayenne pepper with a fork. Add the meatballs.
3. Pour ½ cup water into a steamer or large kettle and place bowl containing egg mixture in water.
4. Bring water to a boil over high heat. Reduce heat to medium, cover pan, and steam for 20 to 25 minutes or until eggs are firm.
5. Serve hot with rice.

Serves 4

Ingredients like tofu, sesame oil, sesame seeds, and cayenne pepper give egg custard with meatballs *(left)* and steamed stuffed peppers *(right)* a **Korean** flavor.

THE CAREFUL COOK

Whenever you cook, there are certain safety rules you must always keep in mind. Even experienced cooks follow these rules when they are in the kitchen.

1. Always wash your hands before handling food.
2. Thoroughly wash all raw vegetables and fruits to remove dirt, chemicals, and insecticides.
3. Use a cutting board when cutting up vegetables and fruits. Don't cut them up in your hand! And be sure to cut in a direction *away* from you and your fingers.
4. Long hair or loose clothing can easily catch fire if brought near the burners of a stove. If you have long hair, tie it back before you start cooking.
5. Turn all pot handles toward the back of the stove so that you will not catch your sleeve or jewelry on them. This is especially important when younger brothers and sisters are around. They could easily knock off a pot and get burned.

6. Always use a pot holder to steady hot pots or to take pans out of the oven. Don't use a wet cloth on a hot pan because the steam it produces could burn you.
7. Lift the lid of a steaming pot with the opening away from you so that you will not get burned.
8. If you get burned, hold the burn under cold running water. Do not put grease or butter on it. Cold water helps to take the heat out, but grease or butter will only keep it in.
9. If grease or cooking oil catches fire, throw baking soda or salt at the bottom of the flame to put it out. (Water will *not* put out a grease fire.) Call for help and try to turn all the stove burners to "off."

METRIC CONVERSION CHART

WHEN YOU KNOW		MULTIPLY BY	TO FIND	
MASS (weight)				
ounces	(oz)	28.0	grams	(g)
pounds	(lb)	0.45	kilograms	(kg)
VOLUME				
teaspoons	(tsp)	5.0	milliliters	(ml)
tablespoons	(Tbsp)	15.0	milliliters	
fluid ounces	(oz)	30.0	milliliters	
cup	(c)	0.24	liters	(l)
pint	(pt)	0.47	liters	
quart	(qt)	0.95	liters	
gallon	(gal)	3.8	liters	
TEMPERATURE				
Fahrenheit temperature	(°F)	5/9 (after subtracting 32)	Celsius temperature	(°C)

COMMON MEASURES AND THEIR EQUIVALENTS

3 teaspoons = 1 tablespoon

8 tablespoons = ½ cup

2 cups = 1 pint

2 pints = 1 quart

4 quarts = 1 gallon

16 ounces = 1 pound

INDEX
(recipes indicated by **bold face** *type)*

ABOUT THE AUTHORS

Okwha Chung was born in South Korea, and she moved to Minneapolis, Minnesota, in 1974. She teaches Sunday school at Minnesota's only Korean school. Chung also enjoys playing the piano and cooking Korean favorites for her family and students.

Judy Monroe, born in Duluth, Minnesota, has mastered several southeast Asian cuisines, including Korean cooking. A graduate of the University of Minnesota, Monroe is currently a biomedical librarian and a freelance writer. She enjoys ethnic cooking, baking, gardening, reading, and playing her folk harp.